DAYS THAT SHOOK THE WORLD

PEARL HARBOR

DECEMBER 7, 1941

Paul Dowswell

RSVP® **RAINTREE STECK-VAUGHN PUBLISHERS**

A Harcourt Company

Austin   New York

www.raintreesteckvaughn.com

DAYS THAT SHOOK THE WORLD

Assassination in Sarajevo	Hiroshima
The Chernobyl Disaster	The Kennedy Assassination
D-Day	The Moon Landing
The Dream of Martin Luther King	Pearl Harbor
The Fall of the Berlin Wall	The Wall Street Crash

Published by Raintree Steck-Vaughn Publishers,
an imprint of Steck-Vaughn Company

Library of Congress Cataloging-in-Publication Data is available upon request.

ISBN 0-7398-6051-8

Printed in Italy. Bound in the United States.

1 2 3 4 5 6 7 8 9 0 LB 06 05 04 03 02

Picture Acknowledgments:

Cover picture: The U.S. battleships *West Virginia* and *Tennessee* under attack by Japanese bombers and midget submarines on December 7, 1941.
Title page picture: Severely damaged, the *West Virginia* (foreground) settles on the bottom of Pearl Harbor.

We are grateful to the following for permission to reproduce photographs:
AKG 8, 12; Associated Press 10, 34 bottom; Corbis front cover (Bettmann), 6 bottom (Edwin Levick), 14 (Pan-Pacific Press), 16 (Bettmann), 17, 18, 23 (Bettmann), 25 (Bettmann), 26 (Bettmann), 27 (Bettmann), 28 left, 29 (Bettmann), 30 bottom, 32 (Bettmann), 33 (Seattle Post-Intelligencer Collection; Museum of History & Industry/CORBIS), 34 top (Bettmann), 37, 39 top, 40, 41, 42 (Hulton-Deutsch Collection); Corbis Stock Market 43 top (Jose Fuste Raga); Hulton Archive 15 top, 20 top, 22 right, 24 (Scott Swanson Collection); Peter Newark's Pictures 2, 6 top, 7, 9, 13 bottom, 19 top, 21, 30 top, 36 top, 43 bottom, 46; Topham Picturepoint 13 top, 19 bottom, 28 right, 31, 36 bottom, 38; TRH 20 bottom, 22 left, 39.

CONTENTS

AT 7:50 A.M. ON A QUIET Sunday morning at Pearl Harbor on Oahu Island, Hawaii, the distant buzz of aircraft engines slowly penetrated the open doors and hatches of the U.S. battleship *Arizona*. The sound drifted down the steel stairs and along narrow corridors to the cramped quarters of the sleeping crewmen. It was not a sound they were used to hearing at this time on a Sunday morning. Saturday night was shore leave night. Those of the *Arizona*'s crew who were awake enough to notice the noise were nursing hangovers, or contemplating a swim, a game of tennis, or maybe even attending a Sunday church service. Men on other ships, and in onshore navy and air force barracks heard the noise too, but most thought nothing more about it.

Life in the American navy at Pearl Harbor in 1941 was as close as anyone gets in the military to a five-day week. Men were often on ship and at sea Monday to Friday, and then had the weekend off to relax. The Japanese intelligence service knew this, too, for they had spies on the island who regularly passed on such information. This was why the Japanese airborne attack force arrived at 7:50 A.M. on a Sunday.

So unprepared were the Americans, that the Japanese aircrews were able to tune into local radio stations and use these to guide themselves toward the island. They could not have picked a better time of the week. So unexpected was the attack that ammunition for U.S. antiaircraft guns was locked away in ship and shore storage lockers.

The U.S.S. *Arizona* plows through the ocean in 1931. Berthed at Pearl Harbor, the battleship would be totally destroyed in the attack ten years later.

Having dropped its bomb load over Pearl Harbor, a Japanese Val aircraft strains to pull out of its dive.

Pearl Harbor a few weeks before the Japanese attack. Neat rows of warships, often grouped in pairs, made virtually unmissable targets.

Circling high above the harbor in a Kate bomber was the attack commander Fuchida Mitsuo. He looked down at the *Arizona*, moored alongside another six mighty battleships that were also berthed there. Also below him lay another 80 or so vessels of the U.S. Pacific fleet. Certain that the arrival of his planes had been a total surprise, Fuchida fired a black flare from the aircraft window. This was the signal to attack. The fate of Pearl Harbor was sealed. In less than two hours, the *Arizona* would be partially sunk, more than 2,400 men would be dead, 180 aircraft would lie in crumpled piles, and 17 other naval ships would be mangled wrecks.

Admiral Yamamoto Isoroku (1884–1943)

Appointed commander-in-chief of the Japanese combined fleet in September 1939, Admiral Yamamoto was the principal architect of the Pearl Harbor attack, and Japan's follow-up strategy. His bold plan envisioned a short war concluding in a Japanese victory, leaving Japan as undisputed master of the Asian Pacific. Yamamoto had spent time in the United States as a diplomat, and was always doubtful that his plan would succeed. He never lived to see the consequences of his attack—the total defeat of Japan. He was killed in 1943 when his aircraft was shot down by U.S. fighter planes.

JAPAN HAD ALWAYS BEEN something of a mystery to westerners—who looked upon the country with a mixture of fear and fascination. Many of those who had lived through World War II, and those growing up in the decade or so following it, found it difficult to forget the seemingly bizarre cruelty of Japanese soldiers during the conflict. Yet the Japanese language and customs and the country's beautiful art and architecture held a strange attraction for many westerners.

The West has often underestimated Japan, and it was such a misjudgment that led directly to Japan's success at Pearl Harbor. For centuries, Japan had cut itself off from foreign contact. While European powers such as Great Britain, France, Holland, and Portugal carved out their own Far Eastern empires in territories such as China, Southeast Asia, and Indonesia, Japan remained out of reach. European traders who approached its forbidden shores were turned away.

However, in 1853, the United States made the Japanese an offer they couldn't refuse. U.S. navy commander Matthew Perry arrived at Edo (now Tokyo) with a fleet of naval steamships. The locals, unfamiliar with western technology, thought these strange ships had "harnessed volcanoes," and were terrified. Perry demanded that the Japanese open their country to western trade. This they did, and Japan forged close ties with both the United States and Great Britain. But Japan was also determined to learn as much as it could from the West. Within half a century, the country had become a modern, industrialized society. Modernization also brought power. Japan's military strength was displayed to the world when the nation beat the Russian fleet off the Tsushima Islands

This American illustration shows Commander Matthew Perry arriving in Japan in July 1853.

during the Russo-Japanese war of 1904–1905. The victory resulted in a humiliating defeat for Russia, and would eventually lead to Japanese control of the disputed territory of Manchuria, which lay on Russia's far-eastern border.

During World War I, Japan fought on the same side as Great Britain, France, and the United States. But after the war, Japan was not treated as the great power it now believed itself to be. The Japanese were particularly displeased that the Treaty of Versailles, signed by the Allies and Germany at the end of the war, refused to recognize the concept of racial equality. During the 1920s and especially the 1930s, many of Japan's political and military leaders began to feel that their natural allies in the West were not the **democracies** of Great Britain and America, but authoritarian regimes such as those of the **Nazis** in Germany and **Fascists** in Italy.

Japan Makes Use of the West

" Knowledge shall be sought all over the world so as to strengthen the foundation of imperial rule. "

From a proclamation made in 1868 by the Japanese emperor.

" The Japanese only look upon foreigners as schoolmasters. As long as they cannot help themselves they make use of them; and then they send them about their business. "

The words of a European visitor to Japan during the late 19th century.

A Japanese artist records Japan's naval victory against the Russian fleet at Tsushima in 1905.

Japanese troops charge into the teeth of a Chinese army bombardment during the invasion of China in August 1937.

I N 1929 THE UNITED STATES' economy almost collapsed and American banks recalled loans (asked for their money back) that they had made to foreign countries. All over the world, businesses failed and people were thrown out of work. Japan was no exception. The effects of the economic crash (known as the Great Depression) prompted a noticeable shift in power. Increasingly, Japan's military leaders assumed control of the country, and army generals began to act independently of government. Many of these military leaders rejected liberal western ideas, and turned instead to the old, traditional Japanese values. The warrior code of **Bushido**, which emphasized duty, obedience, and other military virtues, came to be the dominant official attitude in Japan.

A Moment in Time

In December 1937, Japanese troops seize the Chinese city of Nanking. More than 100,000 people are killed in an orgy of rape, looting, and murder. The massacre is deliberately intended to provoke fear among Japan's neighbors and weaken the resolve of nations to resist her. Similar atrocities mark the seizure of Hong Kong, and other cities, during Japan's conquest of the Pacific and help to cement the idea in the minds of many westerners that the Japanese are a brutal, sadistic people.

Japanese foreign policy became more **nationalistic** and aggressive. In military terms, Japan was surrounded by weaker countries. It had already annexed (taken over) Korea in 1910. A civil war between nationalists and communists divided the country of China, meaning that it posed little threat to Japan's increasing influence in Manchuria (a province of China). Other nearby countries were controlled by declining colonial powers such as the Netherlands (Holland), France, and Great Britain. Japan's masters had a vision of their country emerging as a new leader of a post-colonial Asia.

The United States watched with increasing suspicion. The U.S. was now a colonial power itself in the region, with control of the Philippines. The United States also saw the divided China as a newly emerging political giant, and believed its influence could be used in China to help that country become the world's largest democracy by supporting the nationalists. However, in 1937 Japan invaded China, an act so resented by the United States that economic retaliation followed. Essential U.S. exports of oil and rubber were cut off and Japanese assets in U.S. banks were frozen. The United States' policies pushed Japan directly into a wider war. With few of her own natural resources and a huge and growing population, Japan was placed in a do or die situation. If it wished to continue a policy of expansion, it had to act fast before the supplies needed to wage war ran out. Further expansion could only be guaranteed by seizing nearby territories to gain the essential oil, coal, rubber, and other materials needed to supply Japan's factories and ensure continued prosperity.

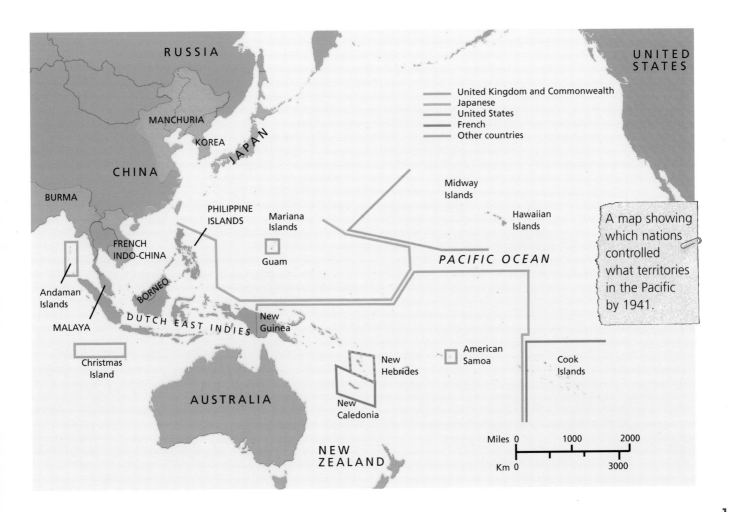

A map showing which nations controlled what territories in the Pacific by 1941.

Hitler and Mussolini (seated next to one another, left and right). The German and Italian dictators thought they had found kindred spirits in the Japanese—but the European and Asian sides of the Axis coalition rarely cooperated.

THE GREAT DEPRESSION HAD terrible consequences in Europe too, where millions of people were thrown out of work. In Germany, Adolf Hitler, leader of the far-right Nazi Party, fed on this tide of human misery and was swept to power in January 1933. Promising his nation prosperity through conquest, he successfully nibbled away at Germany's neighboring territory until his invasion of Poland in 1939 provoked the French and British into war.

Adolf Hitler had an ally in Europe—the Italian dictator Benito Mussolini. Both Hitler and Mussolini were strong, charismatic figures who ruled their countries with an iron will. Both believed that conquest would make them great, and both hated and feared the communist regime of Russia (then known as the Soviet Union).

The rulers of Japan, who also glorified military might and feared the Soviets, had much in common with Germany and Italy. All three countries felt that they were "have not" nations—that they lacked the prosperity-generating empires of European powers such as Great Britain, France, and Holland. In many ways

they were natural allies. Throughout the 1930s they grew closer, until Japan bound itself to the fates of Germany and Italy in the 1940 Tripartite Pact, where it became the third of the so-called "Axis" powers.

However, there were other links between Europe and the wider world that were more uncertain. Great Britain, one of Japan's major rivals for power in the Far East, had a close but unpredictable relationship with the United States. North America had begun her existence as a British colony. Although it had won its independence through a war, there were still strong links with the British, not least in trade and business.

In 1917, the entry of the United States on the side of the British and French into World War I had ensured Germany's defeat. But the war had convinced many Americans that their country should retire from world politics. During the 1930s, "isolationism" was a particularly strong force in the United States. "Let the world fight its wars without America" became a popular slogan. Because of this isolationism, Japan's leaders could not be certain of the United States' reaction to their own increasing power. When, in

1939, war broke out in Europe, U.S. president Franklin D. Roosevelt began supplying Great Britain with arms and other goods in their fight against Germany. Japanese leaders were left to wonder what Roosevelt might do if Japan began to seize the assets of western colonies in the Far East.

In June 1941, Japan's ally Germany invaded the Soviet Union. Japan faced a choice. Should it help the Nazis by attacking the weakened Soviets to the north? Or should the Japanese risk war with the United States and the still undefeated British, by attacking their colonies to the south?

A Special Relationship?

The United States and Great Britain spoke the same language and shared a similar belief in democracy. There were strong cultural links, insofar as the United States had received a large number of British immigrants during the previous 300 years. There were also strong family links: in the late 19th century, many a daughter of a wealthy American industrialist or financier had married a member of the British aristocracy. Winston Churchill, who was to become Britain's prime minister during World War II, was half-American himself, on his mother's side.

German infantrymen, supported by tanks, advance warily into Soviet Russia.

U.S. president Roosevelt and British prime minister Churchill meet for the first time in August 1941.

An official ceremony marking the U.S. annexation of Hawaii in August 1898.

PEARL HARBOR IS A MASSIVE naval base occupying a vast natural inlet in Honolulu County, Oahu Island, Hawaii. It was, and still is, one of the United States' principal bases in the Pacific. In 1941 it was the headquarters of the United States Pacific fleet. Without it, the U.S. navy would have had to oversee the country's Pacific possessions and protect its merchant ships from bases on the west coast of the United States.

Americans first came to Hawaii in the 1820s, when it was an independent monarchy. In 1887, the Americans persuaded the Hawaiians to let them use Pearl Harbor. They built repair workshops there, along with coal refueling stations for their merchant ships and navy. By the early 1890s, American settlers in Hawaii were pressing the United States government to annex the islands; this it finally did in 1898. Now that Hawaii was part of U.S. territory, the government set about making major improvements to Pearl Harbor. It took ten or so years to dredge a wide channel at the mouth of the inlet, removing sand and coral there to a depth of 36 feet (11 m). The inlet as a whole had waters that reached depths of 60 feet (18 m), which made it suitable for the largest battleships.

By the end of World War I, air power had become a third, vital element, alongside the army and navy, in any nation's fighting force. Several airfields were built on Oahu Island for flying boats, bombers, and fighter planes.

Pearl Harbor has hundreds of anchorages for ships, as well as repair workshops and vast fuel stores. On the day of the Japanese attack, more than 80 ships of all shapes and sizes, from destroyers to tugboats, submarines to cruisers, were floating in the harbor. Most crucial of all, berthed side by side, bow to stern, in a section of the inlet known as "Battleship Row," lay seven of the United States' most powerful battleships: U.S.S. *Nevada, Arizona, Tennessee, West Virginia, Maryland, Oklahoma,* and *California*. There were other ships based at Pearl Harbor too, most notably three huge aircraft carriers. Fortunately, on the day of the attack these carriers and their cruiser escorts were out at sea, along with approximately one third of the rest of the Pacific fleet.

Civilian housing, close to the Pearl Harbor base, photographed shortly before the attack in 1941.

The ships docked at Pearl Harbor presented an obvious and easy target, as did much of the air force. As a precaution against sabotage, many aircraft had been gathered together on their airfields in neat, closely packed rows. Laid out in the open and positioned close together, the planes were much easier to guard.

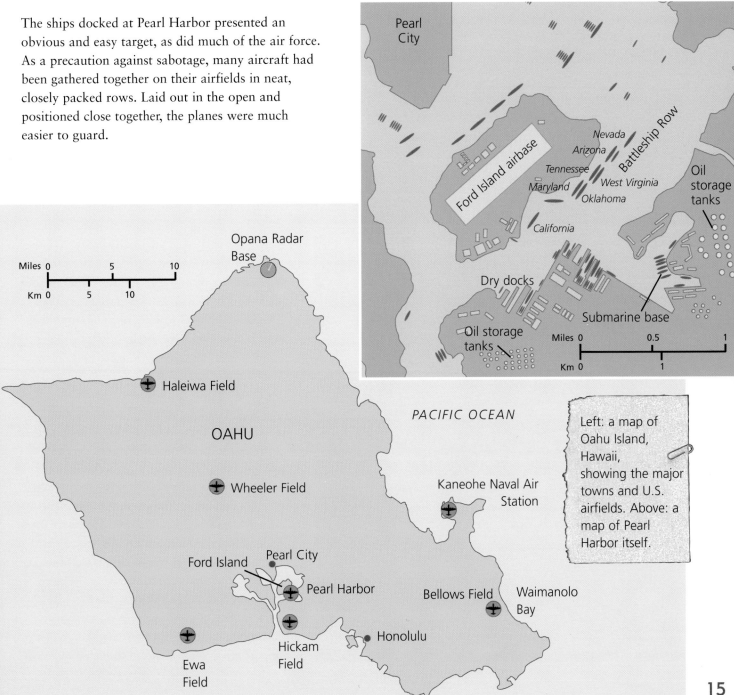

Pearl City

Ford Island airbase

Nevada
Arizona
Tennessee
Maryland
West Virginia
Oklahoma
California

Battleship Row

Oil storage tanks

Dry docks

Submarine base

Oil storage tanks

Miles 0   0.5   1
Km 0   1

Opana Radar Base

Miles 0   5   10
Km 0   5   10

Haleiwa Field

OAHU

Wheeler Field

PACIFIC OCEAN

Kaneohe Naval Air Station

Ford Island

Pearl City

Pearl Harbor

Bellows Field

Waimanolo Bay

Honolulu

Ewa Field

Hickam Field

Left: a map of Oahu Island, Hawaii, showing the major towns and U.S. airfields. Above: a map of Pearl Harbor itself.

15

A plantation worker in Indonesia in the late 1930s makes a cut in the bark of a rubber tree to obtain latex—the raw material used to produce rubber.

By the summer of 1941, Japan was in a very difficult position. The invasion of China had stalled and the army was bogged down in a guerrilla war with Chinese forces. The prospect of invading other countries farther south was tempting, but the chances of success were receding each day. In response to Japan's war with China, Great Britain had joined the United States in imposing trade sanctions. The longer Japan waited to act, the fewer would be its remaining stocks of fuel and other essential supplies that were needed to wage war.

South of Japan, around the eastern shores of the Pacific, lay the colonies of Great Britain and Holland. These colonies were sources of two essential raw materials for war. Rubber and oil were to be found in Malaysia and in the Dutch East Indies (now Indonesia). When Germany conquered France in 1940, the Nazis allowed their Japanese allies to take over the French colony of Indo-China (now Vietnam, Laos, and Cambodia), which made these raw materials all the more accessible. The United States' colony of the Philippines was also within easy reach.

It was a very tempting prospect. If the Japanese struck fast and sure, the Pacific colonies would be theirs. Then, if all went according to plan on other fronts, the Japanese army could invade Great Britain's greatest colony, India. German troops fighting in the Soviet Union and Italian troops fighting in the Middle East could link up with Japanese forces somewhere around Afghanistan or Persia (now Iran). Then the Axis countries would control the oil supplies that would ensure that their armed forces had sufficient fuel.

Even if this did not come to pass, reasoned Japan's military leaders, they would entrench themselves in the conquered countries in Pacific

This picture was frequently used in Allied propaganda to show how a scale model of Pearl Harbor was built to train Japanese pilots for the attack. It was, in fact, a model used in a subsequent Japanese film celebrating the raid.

Asia. Faced with a united front, the western powers would not have the strength or the heart to fight on, and they would make peace.

Japan's greatest problem in achieving this aim was likely to be a military response from Great Britain and the United States. Great Britain, though, was already fighting for its life against the Nazis in Europe. This left the United States. A lightning attack on Pearl Harbor would cripple the U.S. fleet for long enough to allow Japan to seize the territory she wanted in Pacific Asia. It was a bold plan, and it might just work....

Yamamoto's "Wild Show"

" [The Japanese navy will put on] ... a wild show for six months to a year, but if the war drags on to two or three years I cannot be confident of the outcome. "

Admiral Yamamoto's words to the Japanese government in April 1941. Yamamoto was keenly aware of the need for a speedy campaign. He knew that the attack he was planning against the United States was Japan's greatest ever gamble.

" I find my present position extremely strange—forced ... to unswervingly follow a course [of war against the United States] which is exactly the opposite of my personal views. "

Yamamoto's words to a friend in October 1941.

A decisive moment of history frozen in time: Japanese planes prepare to take off from their carrier flight deck for the raid on Pearl Harbor.

UNDER THE ORDERS OF ADMIRAL Yamamoto, the 32 ships that would make up the first aircraft carrier strike force began to assemble in the chilly waters of Hitokappu Bay, north of the Japanese main island. After four days, the fleet was ready. On November 26, under the command of Vice-Admiral Chuichi Nagumo, it began its 3,420-mile (5,500-k) journey to Hawaii.

The December 7th date for the attack was crucial, and had been decided as early as the first week in October. There would be a full moon (important for navigation) on the night of December 6–7, and it was well known that the U.S. navy would be at its least prepared on Sunday morning. A month later there would be seasonal storms in the North Pacific, making such an expedition from Japan all but

Vice-Admiral Chuichi Nagumo, commander of the Pearl Harbor strike force.

A Moment in Time

Dawn has not yet broken on December 7, 1941, but the first light of day gathers in a gray rim along the horizon. Aboard Vice-Admiral Nagumo's carrier *Akagi*, an officer hoists a tattered signal flag for the letter Z. The same flag was used by the Japanese navy in 1905 before the phenomenal Japanese victory over the Russian fleet at Tsushima. It flutters and flaps in the teeth of a cutting sea wind. The other carriers in the fleet note the flag. It is the signal to begin the attack.

As December 6th became December 7th, the fleet had almost reached its launch point. The aircrews were roused from their sleeping quarters at 5:00 A.M. and within an hour were standing on the wind-blown flight decks of their carriers, listening to commanding officers make patriotic speeches, and drinking a toast of *saké* wine. The first aircraft left their carriers at 6:10 A.M. They were 280 miles (450 k) north of Oahu Island. Within fifteen minutes, a first-wave strike force of 183 planes was heading for Hawaii.

impossible. In Southeast Asia too, where Japan hoped its armies would soon win sweeping victories, the best time of year to mount an attack was between October and April, before the monsoon rains came. In early December, time was already running out.

Winter was closing in, and the fleet suffered the worst weather December could provide. There were flurries of snow, fog, and then gales and mountainous seas. The weather was so bad that the voyage would have been canceled if it had been an exercise. But the weather provided excellent cover for the ships, and the fleet sailed undetected across a vast, empty Pacific.

These Japanese planes were photographed overtaking an American bomber on their way to Pearl Harbor.

The first bombs begin to fall on "Battleship Row."

Fuchida Mitsuo, commander of the first wave.

7:48 A.M. Away from the main harbor, at Kaneohe naval air station in west Oahu, the first blow was struck. Japanese Vals and Zekes planes bombed and strafed U.S. aircraft and personnel. During the attack, all of Kaneohe's 33 Catalan flying boats were destroyed or badly damaged.

7:53 A.M. In the skies above Pearl Harbor, Attack Commander Fuchida ordered his radioman to send the coded signal *"Tora! Tora! Tora!"* ("Tiger! Tiger! Tiger!"), meaning that the raid had been a total surprise. Those Pearl Harbor residents already up and about were enjoying a sunny and calm Sunday morning. The aircraft now visible in the sky above them were mistaken for U.S. aircraft returning to Hawaii from carriers out at sea.

7:55 A.M. The attacks began on the harbor, but, even then, the first explosions and alarm calls were thought to be part of a surprise training exercise. Ford Island naval air station, in the center of the inlet, was hit first. Airbases at Ewa and Wheeler Field were also bombed and strafed. U.S. ships

Helena, Utah, Oklahoma, and *Raleigh* were all struck by torpedoes from low-flying Kate bombers. *Oglala* had her hull split open by the explosion on the *Helena.*

8:01 A.M. On Battleship Row, U.S.S. *Nevada, Arizona, California,* and *West Virginia* were torpedoed. Almost 90 percent of all the damage inflicted on U.S. ships occurred within the first ten minutes, most of it caused by torpedoes. Adding to the chaos, just after 8:00 A.M. a flight of eleven B-17 bombers from the U.S. mainland began to arrive at Hickam Field airbase just as it, too, came under attack. Amazingly, only one bomber was destroyed, although another three were badly damaged. Half the total number of the other aircraft at the airbase were also destroyed.

8:04 A.M. Already badly damaged by torpedoes, the *Arizona* was struck by a bomb that dropped straight down one of her funnels and detonated her forward magazine. A huge explosion caused the worst casualties of the day. More than a thousand members of the crew were killed.

Hit by bombs and torpedoes, the *West Virginia* settles on the harbor bottom. Behind her is the battleship *Tennessee,* which escaped with little damage.

8:25 A.M. After further bombing and strafing of airfields, the sky went quiet. Of the 183 Japanese planes involved in the first wave, only nine had been lost and nine damaged. For the moment, the attack ceased. But there was more to come.

All Hell Broke Loose

" It was calm and serene inside the harbour.... The orderly groups of barracks, the wriggling white line of an automobile road...fine objectives of attack in all directions. In line with these, inside the harbour, were important ships of the Pacific fleet, strung out and anchored two ships side by side in an orderly manner. "

Japanese Commander Itaya, quoted in S. E. Morrison's History of the United States Naval Operations in World War Two.

" I suddenly realized these planes were not our own.... Within the next few moments all hell broke loose. Torpedo planes swooped in from almost over my head and started toward 'Battleship Row' dropping their lethal fish.... Men were swimming for their lives in the fire-covered water.... "

Chief Petty Officer Leonard J. Fox, quoted in Dan van der Vat's The Pacific Campaign.

THE AIR ATTACKS ON PEARL HARBOR were such a devastating success, that history seems to have forgotten another aspect of the campaign. Japanese midget submarines were also supposed to strike with similar effectiveness. They didn't. This is their story.

12:00 midnight On December 7 the first of five midget submarines was dispatched from its parent submarine, approximately six miles (ten k) from the entrance to Pearl Harbor. During the next three hours, another four were also unleashed. Each submarine carried a crew of two men, and two torpedoes. Their mission: to gain entry to the harbor, and destroy ships at close range.

3:42 A.M. Two U.S. minesweepers, *Condor* and *Crossbill*, were on joint patrol just outside the harbor entrance. Crew on the *Condor* spotted the trail of a submarine periscope.

3:57 A.M. The *Condor* reported its sighting to the destroyer *Ward*, which came to investigate but could find no evidence of a submarine.

4:58 A.M. The *Condor* and *Crossbill* returned to Pearl Harbor through the entrance gate to the inlet, which was then not closed behind them. The incident was not reported, as there had been several false alarms during the previous few weeks.

6:30 A.M. The *Antares*, another U.S. navy ship that was awaiting permission to enter Pearl Harbor, spotted the conning tower of a submarine just outside the harbor entrance. The destroyer *Ward* was summoned again.

6:37 A.M. The *Ward* opened fire, hit the submarine, then destroyed it with a depth charge.

7:03 A.M. The *Ward* spotted another submarine and destroyed it with another depth charge.

7:40 A.M. The *Ward* radioed a report to headquarters, detailing her actions. Inexplicably, no further action was taken to warn the military forces on Oahu.

8:01 A.M. In the middle of the first air attack, a midget submarine had arrived in Pearl

Left: a Japanese midget submarine of the type used in the Pearl Harbor attack. Above: the minesweeper U.S.S. *Condor*, which first spotted the Japanese submarine attack.

Harbor. Lurking opposite "Battleship Row," it released two torpedoes within three minutes. The first hit the *California*, and the second hit the *West Virginia*. Both battleships had already been hit by Japanese planes.

8:30 A.M. Another midget submarine was spotted in the waters between Pearl City and Ford Island, and sunk.

8:40 A.M. In the lull between the first and second waves of the attack, it was realized that the harbor gate had been left open.

9:50 A.M. The U.S. destroyer *Blue* sank another submarine outside the harbor.

10:04 A.M. The cruiser *St. Louis* destroyed another submarine outside the harbor. All five midget submarines were lost in the attack on Pearl Harbor.

A Moment in Time

Released from submarine I.24 in the early hours of December 7, midget submarine crew Sakamaki Kazuo and Inagaki Kiyoshi soon realize they have problems with their navigation equipment. They become hopelessly lost, and their submarine drifts to Waimanolo Bay on the west side of Oahu. To prevent it from falling into enemy hands, they attempt to destroy the submarine with explosives, but these fail to go off. Inagaki Kiyoshi is drowned, but Sakamaki Kazuo is washed ashore unconscious. He becomes the first Japanese prisoner of World War II, and the only Japanese person to be taken alive during the attack on Pearl Harbor.

The *West Virginia*, seen here in front of the *Tennessee*, was a victim of the submarine attack.

hangars on to the flight decks any faster. Launched between 7:05 A.M. and 7:15 A.M., 167 Vals, Kates, and Zekes made up the second wave of Japanese planes. They began to arrive over Pearl Harbor at around 8:40 A.M. that morning. This time, the military personnel on Oahu were expecting them, and a constant wall of antiaircraft shells from U.S. positions exploded in the sky.

8:50 A.M. Lieutenant-Commander Shimazaki, leader of the second wave, ordered the deployment of his aircraft. Within four minutes, Kate bombers were pounding U.S. airbases, and Val dive-bombers were attacking U.S. naval ships. In the dry dock, the battleship *Pennsylvania* was hit, along with the destroyers *Cassin, Downes,* and *Shaw.*

9:08 A.M. A bomb from a Val hit the *Raleigh*, a light cruiser. It penetrated the ship, puncturing the hull below the waterline, and exploded underwater. It missed the *Raleigh*'s 3,602 gallon (13,638 l) fuel tanks by a mere ten feet (three m).

9:10 A.M. The *Nevada*, hit in the first attack, attempted to sail out to open water. However, she was sinking so fast that the captain decided to run her aground to prevent her from blocking the main harbor exit.

9:25 A.M. Badly hit by Japanese bombs, the destroyer *Shaw* was abandoned. Five minutes later, heat from onboard fires ignited her magazines and she was blown to pieces in a colossal explosion.

10:00 A.M. The remaining crew members of the *Oglala*, including her captain, leaped onto the pier as their ship, which had been hit in the previous attack, capsized at her moorings. At around this time, the last Japanese planes left the skies above Oahu to return to their carriers. Attack Commander Fuchida's Kate bomber, together with its two Zeke escorts, was the last plane to leave.

APPROXIMATELY 25 MINUTES passed before the next attack. Naval mission planners would have preferred a shorter gap between waves, but the carrier aircraft elevators were so slow that it was impossible to move planes from their belowdecks

11:15 A.M. Planes from the second wave began to land on their carriers. By 12:14 P.M., all planes not shot down had been recovered.

Without the essential element of surprise, the second attack was nowhere near as successful as the first. Much less damage was done, at a much greater price. This time 20 of the 167 Japanese planes involved in the attack were lost and 65 were damaged—more than half the planes that took part.

A Moment in Time

In Pearl Harbor's Dry Dock No.1, a hit on the destroyer *Cassin* ruptures her fuel tanks, and burning oil spills over her decks and onto the destroyer *Downes,* berthed right next to her. Harbor personnel attempt to douse the flames by flooding the dry dock, but burning oil floating on top of the gushing torrent of water surrounds the two ships in an intense ring of fire. The magazines in both destroyers are detonated, causing immense damage. The *Cassin* rolls off the blocks upon which it is mounted to keep upright, and comes to rest on the *Downes* at a 45° angle.

U.S.S. *Shaw* is blown apart when fires ignite her magazines.

Nbuo Fujita, one of the pilots who bombed Pearl Harbor, poses proudly beside his plane. Unlike most of those involved in the attack, Fujita survived the war.

ATTACK COMMANDER FUCHIDA'S PLANE touched down aboard the *Akagi*. An ecstatic Fuchida hurried across the flight deck to meet with Vice-Admiral Nagumo. Fuchida was determined to launch a third-wave attack as soon as possible. Nagumo, though, was uncertain. So far they had been lucky, but he did not want to turn a triumph into a tragedy. Admiral Yamamoto was consulted by radio, and he supported Nagumo's view.

Over the years, this fateful decision has been seen as a major missed opportunity to inflict further damage on Pearl Harbor. Although scores of ships had already been sunk and damaged, the harbor's repair shops, docks, power stations, and huge fuel reserves (4,500,000 barrels) remained untouched. Had these been destroyed, then the U.S. fleet would have had to fight the war from its main bases on the west coast of America, more than 1,865 miles (3,000 k) farther away from Japan than Pearl Harbor.

So was a third strike feasible? The last aircraft from the second strike landed at 12:15 P.M. There were insufficient reserve planes for an immediate third strike, so existing planes would have had to be refueled, re-armed, and repaired. Crews, too, needed to be debriefed and briefed again. The whole process would have taken maybe three hours. The third strike would not have taken off before 3:00 P.M., nor returned before 7:00 P.M.

Sunset that day was shortly after 5:00 P.M., so it would have been completely dark by 6:00 P.M. In 1941, aircraft did not have the sophisticated navigational devices they have today, and night landings on aircraft carriers were extremely dangerous. Nagumo did not want to risk losing many of his highly trained aircrews right at the start of the war. Besides, by the time the second wave attacked, the

You damned!
Go to the devil!

聞ケ！！
断末魔ノ
豪
鹿
芽
眼
了
晒
影

This bizarre relic from the war shows a propaganda leaflet, intended to be dropped by Japanese planes during the Pearl Harbor attack.

Americans had already geared up their defenses and antiaircraft fire was fierce. A third attack was almost certain to be met by more force, and result in greater losses. Yamamoto's message of support for Nagumo was the deciding factor. At 1:30 P.M. the Japanese strike force turned west to begin its journey home.

It could be argued that it wasn't the lack of a third strike that was the wasted opportunity, but rather the inadequate planning of the first and second strikes. If the first strike had eliminated the essential shore facilities, especially the fuel reserves, and the second strike had attacked the ships, then perhaps a third strike would not have been necessary.

Another Day?

If it was impossible to mount another attack on December 7, then why did Nagumo not launch a third strike the next day? This is a question that has puzzled a number of military analysts. But a third attack would have been ill-advised, for the following reasons:

- Nagumo's supplies were limited. Fuel for his destroyer escorts was in very short supply. Without these escorts, the carriers would have been vulnerable to a U.S. counterattack.

- The U.S. military were searching for his fleet. Staying an extra day would have increased their chances of finding it.

- Only 29 Japanese planes had been lost, but a further 74 had been badly damaged. A third attack would have been mounted by a considerably weakened strike force.

27

As the stragglers from the second attack wave made their way back to the carrier force, the military personnel at Pearl Harbor surveyed the carnage the planes had left behind. The attack had been devastating and the Japanese were jubilant. One U.S. civilian who fell into Japanese hands at the start of the war recalls being greeted by a smiling Japanese naval captain, who told her smugly: "So sorry to tell you—your fleet all sunk."

However, the Japanese were wrong to be so triumphant. Their attack had proved once and for all how effective carrier-based aircraft could be. It was fortunate for the United States that their Pacific fleet carrier force was out at sea when the Japanese pounced. The carrier force was the United States' greatest asset, and it was untouched by the attack.

Even the damage done at Pearl Harbor was not as bad as it looked. True, the *Arizona* and its crew had been destroyed in one blinding instant, and the *Oklahoma* had capsized and was eventually sold for scrap. The target ship *Utah*, already written off as too old to be a fighting vessel, was also sunk. But thanks to the clear thinking and quick actions of their crews, other battleships sunk had been deliberately flooded to ensure that they settled evenly on the shallow harbor bottom, with their upper decks still above water. Within five months, the *California*, *West Virginia*, and *Nevada* were all refloated, repaired, and modernized, and went on to serve throughout the war.

The *Arizona*, where the worst casualties of the day were inflicted, photographed in 1961, twenty years after the attack.

In the hours following the attack, American sailors survey the damage aboard the U.S.S. *Cassin* (left) and U.S.S. *Downes* (right).

All the other ships sunk or damaged on that day were also refloated and repaired. In total, fifteen U.S. navy ships were put out of use for anything up to fifteen months, but in the long run the Japanese had only succeeded in destroying two U.S. battleships. Even this was no great triumph. Both *Arizona* and *Oklahoma* were old-fashioned vessels, and in need of modernization.

The casualties at Pearl Harbor were a terrible tragedy for those who lost family and friends. The sense of outrage among Americans was all the greater for the fact that the attack took place before war had been declared. But compared with other events of World War II the losses were few. Between 1941 and 1945, more than 19,000 Soviets lost their lives each day in the war against Nazi Germany. Set against appalling casualties such as these, the total number of 2,403 killed on December 7 at Pearl Harbor seems slight.

American Losses at Pearl Harbor

18 warships sunk or damaged
2,008 U.S. navy personnel killed
710 wounded
109 Marines killed
69 wounded
218 army personnel killed
364 wounded
Total: 2,335 killed
             1,143 wounded

Civilian casualties
68 killed
35 wounded

Aircraft
97 naval aircraft destroyed
77 army aircraft destroyed
121 damaged

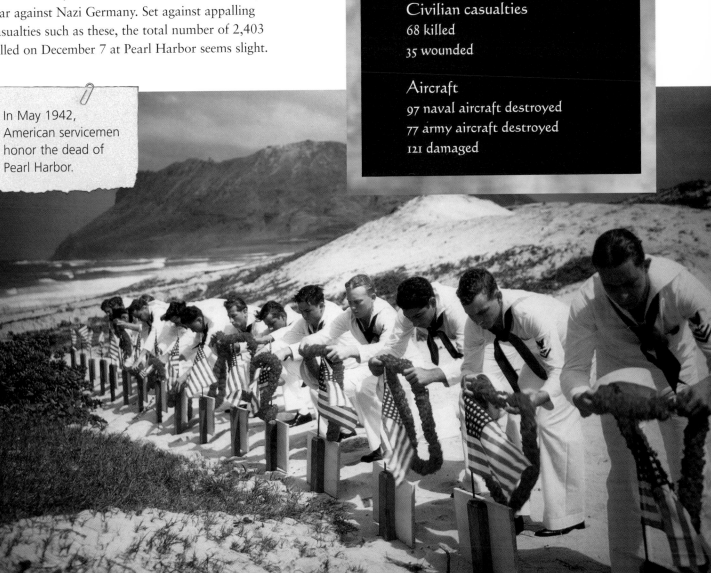

In May 1942, American servicemen honor the dead of Pearl Harbor.

U.S. president Franklin D. Roosevelt, photographed at the White House, Washington, D.C., in 1939.

WITH HINDSIGHT, THE FACT that the United States was so unprepared for the surprise attack at Pearl Harbor is shocking. On the morning of December 7, for example, one third of the ship's officers were on shore leave, no antiaircraft batteries were manned, and ammunition for these vital air defense weapons was even locked up in stores away from the guns. The success of the Japanese onslaught has fueled suspicions that President Roosevelt knew an attack was imminent, but allowed it to happen anyway, to give himself an excuse to bring the United States into a war that the American population did not want.

Today, most historians dismiss this theory as clever propaganda circulated by Republican enemies of the Democrat President Roosevelt. But it is clear that communications between the U.S. navy, army, and the government were very poor, and the information that the U.S. government had of Japanese intentions was woefully mishandled.

The remains of a Navy Scout observation aircraft at Honolulu, just one of the 174 U.S. warplanes destroyed in the attack.

In 1941, the United States had a great advantage over Japan. It knew the secret codes Japan used to communicate both with its overseas embassies and with its armed forces. In the week before the attack, Japanese embassy staff in the United States were told to burn their code books—a sure sign that the Japanese expected war to break out at any moment. Because of this, on November 27, U.S. navy and army commanders received a "war warning" from the U.S. government, telling them that a Japanese attack was imminent.

However, what the Americans did not know was where the Japanese would strike. The U.S. colony of the Philippines was thought to be the most likely target. Any attack on Pearl Harbor, if it came, was expected to be low key—sabotage, perhaps, or a submarine attack. This is why many U.S. aircraft were placed in neat rows in the middle of their runways. They were easy to guard from saboteurs. In the unlikely event of a full-scale attack, Admiral Kimmel, the U.S. navy commander at Pearl Harbor,

assumed that it would come from Japan's Marshall Islands, 2,020 miles (3,250 k) southwest of Hawaii. Air reconnaissance patrols combed that area of the Pacific, but not the north, which was where the Japanese carrier fleet actually came from.

On the day itself, U.S. defenses failed to pick up last-minute warnings of the imminent attack. This failure could be ascribed to incompetence and bad luck. The sighting and sinking of a Japanese miniature submarine at 6:45 A.M. did not raise any alarm and, when approaching Japanese planes were detected by radar at 7:02 A.M., they were thought to be an incoming flight of U.S. bombers.

A Moment in Time

In August 1941, Yugoslavian double-agent Dusko Popov visits New York to inform the U.S. Federal Bureau of Investigation (FBI) of the forthcoming attack at Pearl Harbor. He has fooled the Nazis into thinking he is working for their secret service, and he has access to both German and Japanese military secrets. Expecting to be congratulated for saving American lives on a grand scale, Popov receives the following stunning dismissal: "Your information is too precise. It spells out exactly where, when, how, and by whom we are to be attacked. If anything, it sounds like a trap."

Admiral Kimmel, the U.S. navy commander at Pearl Harbor, misjudged the direction of the attack.

THE MOST IMMEDIATE EFFECT of the attack was that U.S. citizens, willing and unwilling, found themselves at war with Japan. On December 8, President Roosevelt spoke to the nation, describing December 7 as "a date that will live in infamy" and the attack as "unprovoked and dastardly." Later that day, the U.S. Congress passed Public Law 328, which declared that "the President is hereby authorized and directed to employ the entire naval and military forces of the United States and the resources of the Government to carry on war against the Imperial Government of Japan."

Once they had recovered from the initial shock, many Americans felt a cold anger at the attack. Surveying the damage at Pearl Harbor, U.S. navy vice-admiral William F. Halsey Jr. said: "Before we're through with them, the Japanese language will be spoken only in hell!" But this anger could be indiscriminate. There were many people of Japanese extraction in the United States. Most had been there for many years and were loyal Americans. But around 100,000 of them were rounded up and put in detention camps, and had their businesses and property confiscated. The main reason for this was that the U.S. government feared that some Japanese-Americans might aid the enemy in the event of an invasion, or spy for their country of origin. But there was no evidence for this. Toward the end of the war some Japanese-American men were even conscripted to fight for the Allies, and were sent from their detention camps to the war in Europe.

The other direct consequence of the attack was that Germany, Japan's ally, also declared war on the United States, even though there was no obligation for Hitler to do so. Events had played into President Roosevelt's hands. He was not an isolationist—he believed that his country's best interests would be served by actively protecting the United States' allies and possessions. He had been certain that the American population would not go willingly to war against Hitler. Up until this point, he had supported the British with military aid in their struggle. Hitler's declaration of war made everything much simpler. On December 8, Roosevelt sent a telegram to Winston Churchill saying: "Today all of us are in the same boat with you and the people of the Empire, and it is a ship that will not and cannot be sunk."

U.S. sailors read about Pearl Harbor, and the Japanese attack on the Philippines.

These families were among the 100,000 Japanese-Americans interned following Pearl Harbor. Here, a Japanese-American man speaks to fellow internees at the relocation camp in Puyallup, Washington.

The United States in Shock

" Mixed with American fury ... grief ... [and] determination to gain revenge ... was a curious sense of outrage .... America tended to think of the Japanese as an amiable, polite ... race who made good man-servants. "

Historian John Winton in his book War in the Pacific.

" [It was] silent as the grave ... everybody not speaking. Even the people sitting at the eating places, the restaurants, not speaking to each other and looking into the dim distance, absolutely stunned. It was like visiting a drugged nation. "

An English visitor to Chicago describes the main railway station on the day of the attack, quoted in An Ocean Apart by David Dimbleby and David Reynolds.

Japanese army personnel give a victorious cheer in front of a U.S. gun position at Bataan in the Philippines.

ADMIRAL YAMAMOTO HAD PROMISED Japan's military leaders "a wild six months to a year." Once the blow against the United States was struck, it was essential for Japan to act quickly, and unleash her army upon the world. This the Japanese did with murderous efficiency. By the summer of 1942, nearly the whole of the eastern Pacific seaboard was in Japanese hands, as well as the Philippines, Malaya, Thailand, and Burma. India and Australia braced themselves for invasion.

Japanese success was the result of a combination of factors: For the moment, their navy controlled the sea; the European colonial powers they fought had poor air defenses; and, not least, the Japanese army fought with an unbeatable ferocity, sometimes defeating opponents who outnumbered them by two to one.

Prisoners of war were treated with great cruelty by their Japanese captors. At least 7,000 POWs died on the infamous Bataan Death March. This photo shows captured U.S. and Philippine soldiers on the march in April 1942.

Japanese propaganda named the new Empire the "Greater East Asian Co-Prosperity Sphere," and called for "Asia for the Asians." However, as the newly conquered nations quickly discovered, Japan was no better, and often worse, than the Europeans who had formerly ruled over them. The Japanese army, in particular, acted with great cruelty both against the civilian populations it enslaved and the captured soldiers of the armies it routed.

Japanese military conduct ruled that capture was the greatest disgrace, and that every soldier should fight to the death. Although their opponents often fought with great bravery, they would surrender if the battle seemed lost. In Japanese eyes this was an act of craven cowardice. Subsequently, allied prisoners of war were treated with great contempt and cruelty.

Initially, Japan had planned on seizing specific territory, going on the defensive, then making a compromise peace with the United States and Great Britain. But devastating Japanese successes caused military leaders to overextend themselves, and they embarked on invasions of New Guinea, the central Pacific, and even the Aleutian Islands off Alaska. Here Japan suffered her first defeats. Naval battles in the Coral Sea in May 1942, and Midway a month later, saw major losses. (At Midway, Japan lost four vital carriers in two days.)

Ultimately, the ferocity of Japan's fighting forces was no match for U.S. military strength. The Japanese government had underestimated the vengeful anger that the attack on Pearl Harbor had unleashed, and the resolve of the United States to drive Japanese forces from their recently conquered territories.

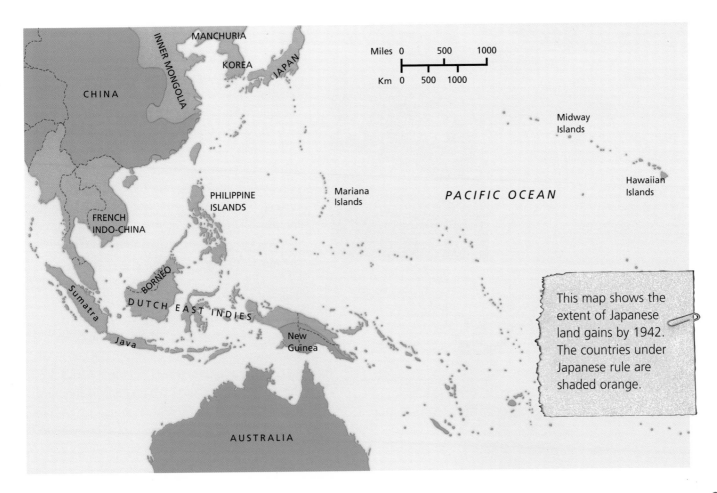

This map shows the extent of Japanese land gains by 1942. The countries under Japanese rule are shaded orange.

35

The key to U.S. success was its phenomenal fighting power. These Dauntless dive bombers were assembled in the hundreds at Douglas Aircraft Plant, Long Beach, California.

A British soldier captures a German tank in the Middle East. British success against the Germans here ensured that German and Japanese troops would never link up.

I N RESPONSE TO THE congratulations offered to him by fellow officers, the architect of the attack, Admiral Yamamoto, said: "I fear that we have only succeeded in awakening a sleeping tiger." He was right. Shocked into action, the United States directed its hugely powerful economy to the task of winning the war. Between 1942 and the war's end in August 1945, U.S. shipyards produced 1,200 new fighting ships (ranging from 18 fleet carriers to 420 destroyer escorts). Such numbers made the losses at Pearl Harbor seem negligible. So did the nation's ability to build new aircraft. By 1944, American factories were producing one new warplane every five minutes.

Although the Pearl Harbor attack came at the end of 1941, the war in the Pacific had been raging since the Japanese invasion of China in 1937. The attack at Pearl Harbor linked the Pacific war with the European war. Japan went to war against Great Britain, which was also fighting Hitler, and Germany declared war on the United States. The attack turned two separate wars about two separate issues into one truly world war. For Japan, it was a tremendous gamble that did not pay off. The triumph of the day, and of Japan's extraordinary advance through Pacific Asia, was short-lived. Within six months, the Japanese navy suffered stunning defeats. For the Imperial Japanese government, the tide turned against them all too soon.

The failure of the Japanese army to advance into India, or gain control of the Indian Ocean against the British navy, stopped them from expanding farther west. Likewise, the defeat of German and Italian armies in North Africa, and then at Stalingrad (now Volgograd) in southern Russia, meant that there was no link-up of Axis forces in the oil-rich Middle East. Throughout the war Germany, Italy, and Japan were all severely hindered by a shortage of fuel.

Hitler's bizarre decision to declare war on the United States following the Pearl Harbor attack guaranteed that U.S. soldiers would fight alongside British, Commonwealth, and French troops at D-Day on June 6, 1944. The D-Day landings on the French coast led to the eventual liberation of Western Europe from the Nazis. That the D-Day landings could have taken place without the massive military strength of the United States is highly unlikely.

U.S. troops and equipment are ferried ashore at Omaha Beach in Normandy, France, shortly after the first successful landings at D-Day.

The Aftereffects of Pearl Harbor

" So we had won the war after all. Our history would not come to an end.... Hitler's fate was sealed. Mussolini's fate was sealed. As for the Japanese, they would be ground to powder. All the rest was merely the proper application of overwhelming force. "

In his memoirs, Winston Churchill recalls his thoughts on hearing that the United States was now at war with both Japan and Germany.

URING THE NEXT THREE-and-a-half years, the United States and her allies fought a slow but steady campaign to clear the Japanese from the territory they had so spectacularly acquired during the first six months of the war. The Japanese held on to their conquests with a dogged determination. U.S. marines, fighting a force of 5,000 Imperial army soldiers at Tarawa atoll in the South Pacific, for example, could only claim the island as their own when the final seventeen defenders surrendered.

As US forces neared the Japanese mainland, the resistance became even more fanatical. At sea, kamikaze pilots attacked U.S. ships, especially aircraft carriers. Kamikazes were often very young men, with little training, who would deliberately fly their explosive-laden planes on suicide missions into U.S. ships.

This formidable resistance, and the extreme difficulties U.S. soldiers experienced as they captured the Japanese island territories of Okinawa and Iwo Jima, led the Americans to deploy a terrible new weapon. On August 6, 1945, a B-29 Superfortress aircraft dropped a single bomb on the Japanese port of Hiroshima. It exploded in a blinding flash of heat and light that killed 80,000 people in an instant. Hitherto untouched by bombing, the city had become the target for the world's first atomic bomb.

The new U.S. president, Harry S. Truman, had decided that fewer lives would be lost if the United States used this enormously destructive weapon to force Japan to surrender. At first, the Japanese were too stunned and disorganized to respond. So, on August 9, 1945, an atomic bomb was also dropped on the city of Nagasaki, causing similar casualties. On August 15, 1945, Japan surrendered, an act that was formalized at a ceremony on board the U.S. navy battleship *Missouri* on September 2. The attack on Pearl Harbor had led to Japan's utter destruction as a military power and the death of two-and-a-quarter million of its soldiers and citizens.

Under sniper fire, U.S. marines take part in grueling jungle fighting at Okinawa in 1945.

One of the most famous images of World War II—U.S. marines raise their flag on Iwo Jima island, en route to Japan.

The Atomic Bomb

"I could not understand why our surroundings had changed so greatly in one instant. I thought it might have been something which had nothing to do with the war, the collapse of the world which it was said would take place at the end of the world."

Hiroshima citizen, Ota Yoko.

An End to War

"It is my earnest hope...that from this solemn occasion a better world shall emerge out of the blood and carnage of the past, a world founded upon faith and understanding, a world dedicated to the dignity of man and the fulfillment of his most cherished wish for freedom, tolerance, and justice.... Let us pray that peace be now restored to the world, and that God will preserve it always. These proceedings are closed."

From General MacArthur's closing speech at the surrender ceremony on board the U.S.S. Missouri.

American sailors crane their necks to view the Japanese surrender aboard the U.S.S. *Missouri*.

A Nazi soldiers strides across the Russian landscape. Behind him, a Soviet ammunition dump blazes away.

Hᴉꜱᴛᴏʀʏ ɪꜱ ꜰᴜʟʟ ᴏꜰ "What ifs?" Such speculation is fascinating, if not very useful. History often turns on a single event which may cause other, hitherto undreamed-of, possibilities and chances to arise in a way that is impossible to predict.

In 1941 there were several clear choices facing Japan's leaders—and at this critical point they made the wrong decision. These same men knew that they had lost the war at least a year before it ended, and their struggle turned from one of conquest to a desperate defense of their country. In the dark months before Japan's total defeat, its leaders must have searched their souls and wondered why they had chosen a course of action that had delivered such a disastrous fate to their nation.

What if Japan had joined Nazi Germany in an attack on the Soviet Union? This may have led to the defeat of Soviet Russia and the triumph of the Axis powers. From the French Atlantic to the Russian Pacific, the Axis alliance would have controlled the greatest landmass of any empire ever. Even without Japanese help, Hitler's armies had reached the gates of Moscow and Leningrad (now St. Petersburg) within weeks of their invasion in June 1941, and the Soviets only survived by sheer determination. If the Russian armies had been forced to fight a two-front war against the Germans in the west and the Japanese in the east, it is likely that the Soviets would have been defeated. Then the Nazis would have ruled over Europe: Hitler would have provided his people with *Lebensraum* (living space) in the east, the Poles and Russians would have

The Nazis treated conquered countries with great cruelty. Here the village of Lidice, Czechoslovakia, is being burned to the ground in retaliation for the murder of two German officers. The men of the village were shot, and the women and children were sent to concentration camps.

A Moment in Time

In February 1941, alone in his study at Nazi headquarters, the German dictator Adolf Hitler studies a large globe. The invasion of Soviet Russia has yet to occur, but plans are well underway. Hitler spins the globe around until the huge landmass of Russia faces him, from one side of the sphere to the other. He takes a pencil and draws a line north to south through the Ural Mountains—the divide between European and Asiatic Russia. West is for Germany, he decides, East is for Japan.

become slave peoples and the Jews in Europe would have been utterly exterminated.

What if Japan had attacked only British and other European colonial possessions? This may well have saved it from suffering a crushing military defeat at the hands of the United States. While President Roosevelt may have seen aggression against U.S. allies as a cast-iron reason for the United States to become involved in the war, there was no guarantee that the American government would have backed him. Without the attack, the United States may never have become involved in the war against Hitler in Europe. Perhaps Great Britain would have survived alone? Perhaps—but if Russia had been overcome by the Axis powers, it is impossible to imagine Great Britain defeating Germany without U.S. help.

The Nazis believed that some nations should be slaves to others and that some ethnic people—for example, Jews and Gypsies—should be wiped out. Today we live in a world where the greatest powers claim, for better or worse and to a greater or lesser extent, to believe in freedom and democracy. If, after World War II, we had found ourselves living in a world run by militaristic Japan and Nazi Germany, it would undoubtedly have been a darker, more sinister place.

IN MANY WAYS THE legacy of Pearl Harbor is indivisible from the legacy of World War II. Along with Hitler's invasion of the Soviet Union, it was one of the most important events of the conflict. Because of what happened at Pearl Harbor, Japan and Germany were defeated by the three strongest military powers in the world—the United States, the Soviet Union, and Great Britain and its Empire.

The war exhausted Great Britain. In the decades that followed, the British Empire, which had included a quarter of the world's population, dissolved. Countries once ruled by Great Britain, including India, Burma, Malaya, Singapore, British Borneo, and British New Guinea, so recently regained from Japan, declared their independence. In place of Empire, a more informal association of states linked with Great Britain, known as the British Commonwealth, emerged.

After the war, U.S. and British Commonwealth forces occupied Japan. This occupation formally ended in 1952, following the setting up of a democratic system of government. Japan recovered from its defeat remarkably quickly. Where wooden cities once lay in ruins there are now gleaming skyscrapers, and its economy became one of the strongest in the world. Having failed to prosper by military strength, Japan has grown wealthy on an extraordinary post-war economic success, which has filled virtually every western household with at least one Japanese television, video, or sound system.

World War II made the capitalist United States and communist Soviet Union the most powerful countries in the world. But, with their common enemies defeated, relations between them soon turned very frosty. The Cold War began. Both sides possessed atomic weapons hundreds of times more powerful than those dropped on Japan, and there was a very real possibility that they would be used against one another in anger. Pearl Harbor, then and now still the headquarters of the U.S. Pacific fleet, was a vital staging post for U.S. troops heading for the Korean War (1950–1953) and the Vietnam War (1964–1975) —both key conflicts in America's fight against communism. The collapse of the Soviet Union in 1991 led to the emergence of the United States as the world's sole great superpower.

For 60 years the Pearl Harbor attack has lived up to President Roosevelt's description as a "date that will live in infamy." It has been invoked to remind Americans about the consequences of treachery by foreign powers and complacency in government. The United States' foreign policy has been based on the thinking "No more Pearl Harbors" ever since.

An occupying American sailor goes souvenir shopping in Tokyo, 1945. In the absence of display windows, goods were sold on the sidewalk of the streets of Tokyo.

The skyline of modern Tokyo. Today, Japan is one of the world's wealthiest nations.

The wreck of the U.S.S. *Arizona* today, with its concrete and steel memorial building.

A Moment in Time

In September 2002, a visitor strolling along the wharves at Pearl Harbor sees that, of all the battleships berthed there on December 7, 1941, only the charred wreck of the U.S.S. *Arizona* remains. Covered by a white concrete and steel sheath, the ship is now a national memorial.

Next to the *Arizona*, on the harbor front, is the battleship *Missouri*, on whose deck Japan signed the documents of surrender. Here together are the beginning and the end of the United States' involvement in World War II.

Glossary

air reconnaissance To observe an enemy's bases or movements from an aircraft.

aircraft carrier A ship that carries military aircraft.

anchorage The place where a ship is positioned in a harbor.

antiaircraft shell An explosive device fired at aircraft.

assets Land or raw materials owned by a country.

atoll A small island made of coral.

authoritarian regime A form of government that insists on strict obedience to its rule.

Axis powers The alliance of Nazi Germany, Japan, and Fascist Italy during World War II.

B-29 Superfortress aircraft A large four-engine long-range American bomber.

barracks Accommodation for military personnel.

battleship A large, heavily armed and armored warship.

Bushido A code of conduct for Japanese warriors, originating in medieval times, stressing courage, loyalty, and self-discipline.

capitalist A person who believes in capitalism, an economic system where factories and other businesses and property are owned by individuals, rather than by the state.

Catalan flying boat A U.S. two-engine plane that can land and take off on water.

charismatic Used to describe a personal quality that enables a person to inspire or influence other people.

colonial To do with colonies.

colony A country controlled by another country.

Commonwealth In this case, an informal alliance of Great Britain and countries that used to be part of the British Empire.

communist A person who believes in communism, an economic system where the state controls wealth and industry supposedly on behalf of the people.

conning tower The tower-like structure on top of a submarine.

cruiser A high-speed warship, with medium arms and armor.

democracy The rule of a country by a government elected by the people.

Democrat A member or supporter of one of the two main U.S. political parties.

depth charge An antisubmarine device, set to explode at a particular depth of water.

destroyer A small, fast, lightly armored warship.

detention camp A place where people, usually civilians, are held prisoner.

diplomat A member of a government whose job entails dealing with the representatives of governments of other countries.

dry dock The section of a harbor that can be drained of water, and where a ship can be placed for repair.

empire Lands and peoples ruled over by another land.

exports Goods sold to a foreign country or countries.

Fascist A person who believes in fascism, a political philosophy that is very conservative, having one unquestioned leader, and nationalist policies.

guerrilla A member of an informal armed force, usually fighting a stronger regular army by hit-and-run tactics.

immigrant A person settled in a country other than that of his/her birth.

infamy Having a reputation for evil.

isolationism A policy of withdrawal from international affairs.

Kate The U.S. code word for the Japanese Kakajima B5NI bomber.

liberal A person or party with political views that favor tolerance of others and personal freedom.

magazine The section of a weapon or ship that contains bullets or shells.

merchant ship A ship that carries cargo.

midget submarine A small submarine operated by one or two crew members.

minesweeper A ship that removes enemy mines from the sea.

nationalist A person who staunchly supports their own country.

nationalistic Putting one's own country first, no matter what the rights or wrongs of the situation.

naval air station An airfield controlled by a navy.

Nazi A member of the political party lead by Adolf Hitler, which was violently opposed to Jews and communism, and which believed in the destiny of Germany to rule the world.

Republican A member or supporter of one of the two main U.S. political parties.

sabotage The destruction of equipment by secret means.

saboteur A person who commits acts of sabotage.

strafe To attack with machine gun fire, usually from a low-flying plane.

submarine A vessel that can travel under water, and which is usually armed with torpedoes.

trade sanctions Measures taken by a country that forbid the export or import of goods to or from another country.

Val The U.S. code word for the Japanese Aichi D3AI Type 99 dive-bomber.

Zeke The U.S. code word for the Japanese Mitsubishi A6M2 Type 00 Zero fighter plane.

Further Information

Reading

Allen, Thomas B. *Remember Pearl Harbor: American and Japanese Survivors Tell Their Stories.* Washington, D.C.: National Geographic Society, 2001.

Anthony, Nathan. *The Bombing of Pearl Harbor in American History (In American History).* Berkeley Heights, NJ: Enslow Publishers Inc., 2001.

Denenberg, Barry. *Early Sunday Morning: The Pearl Harbor Diary of Amber Billows, Hawaii, 1941 (Dear Diary).* New York: Scholastic Trade, 2001.

Dowswell, Paul. *Twentieth-Century Perspectives: The Cause of World War Two.* Chicago, IL: Heinemann Library, 2002.

McGowen, Tom. *The Attack on Pearl Harbor (Conerstones of Freedom).* Danbury, CT: Children's Press, 2002.

Streissguth, Thomas. *The Attack on Pearl Harbor (At Issue in History).* San Diego, CA: Greenhaven Press Inc., 2001.

Tanaka, Shelley. *Attack on Pearl Harbor: The True Story of the Day America Entered World War II.* New York: Hyperion Press, 2001.

Films

Beyond the Movies—Pearl Harbor. National Geographic, 2001.

National Geographic's Ultimate WWII Collection (Untold Stories/The Battle for Midway/ Pearl Harbor: Legacy of Attack). National Geographic, 2002.

Pearl Harbor. Walt Disney Home Video, 2001.

War Stories: Remembering Pearl Harbor. Arcorn Media, 1991.

Time Line

1853 Matthew Perry leads U.S. fleet to Japan, to demand trade between Japan and Western nations.

1887 Pearl Harbor first used as a navy base by the United States.

1904-1905 Japan defeats Russia in the Russo-Japanese War.

1910 Japan annexes neighboring Korea.

1929 The Wall Street Crash signals the beginning of the Great Depression.

1931 Japan invades the Chinese province of Manchuria, and sets up puppet state of Manchukuo.

1933 Hitler and the Nazi Party come to power in Germany.

1937 Japan invades China.

1939 War begins in Europe as Germany invades Poland.

1940 Japan becomes the third member of the "Axis" coalition, along with Nazi Germany and Fascist Italy.

June 22, 1941 Germany invades Soviet Russia.

December 7, 1941 Pearl Harbor attacked by Japanese.

December 8, 1941 United States declares war on Japan. Germany declares war on United States.

December 1941–June 1942 Japan invades the countries of the Asian Pacific Rim and Pacific Islands.

May 1942 Battle of Coral Sea—first Japanese defeat at hands of U.S. navy.

June 1942 Battle of Midway—second Japanese defeat at hands of U.S. navy.

August 6, 1945 U.S. drops atomic bomb on Hiroshima.

August 9, 1945 U.S. drops atomic bomb on Nagasaki.

August 15, 1945 Japan surrenders.

1952 U.S. occupation of Japan comes to an end.

Pearl Harbor on December 7, 1941.

Index